M000223383

Find Your
MAGIC

CREATE *the* MAGICAL LIFE *of Your* DREAMS

THROUGH INTENTION SETTING AND
FOLLOWING YOUR PATH TO JOY

FORTUNA NOIR

ILLUSTRATED BY SELCHA UNI

ROCK
POINT

The Magical World Around You

Nature is all around us. Even if we are not surrounded by greenery, she is still with us in the air we breathe and the sunlight shining on us. She speaks to us with the breeze, beckons us with the lushness of the forest. And when she calls, we listen. Witchcraft is primarily a Nature-based practice. We let the phases of the Moon, changing of the seasons, and our own internal compass guide us. Like the earth, we live through many periods of birth, maturity, and then death. Life is about growth, pruning away what does not serve us, and cycles of rest and action. There is no "one life to live" but instead many small lifetimes in the wonder that is you.

In this journal, you will meditate with goddesses of adventure and kindness. You will dance like the witches who created the Witches' Ring. And you will discover that snakes are not nearly as frightening as they seem. If taken seriously, these journeys will help you understand yourself and the earth in a different way. Let the Crone and her wisdom guide you. Allow the Sun to provide what you need. Let go of distraction and replace it with mindfulness.

Meditation is the practice of sitting in stillness and letting your mind process what it needs to. It has many benefits, like mitigating anxiety, promoting tranquility, and bringing us closer to the divine. When we are saddled with the duties of the material world, we may lose ourselves in the stress of life rather than take care of ourselves the way we deserve. Behind the madness are beautiful things waiting to be discovered.

When we give ourselves the chance to mature and see who we truly are, we flourish. There is nothing more precious than knowing who we are and moving about the world with that confidence. It is my hope that within the pages of this journal, you will find the keys that will transform you as a witch and alter your soul. Now you can begin your meditative journey. The world is waiting for the new you.

ON THE PATH OF
MINDFULNESS
and SELF-CARE

This journal contains seasonal meditations to help you unwind and reflect in your free time. Each meditation is followed by writing prompts to help you dig deeper into your thoughts, feelings, dreams, and personal growth. Each prompt is meant to guide you into nurturing your authentic self through reflection, manifestation, and letting go of what is holding you back. Because of our high-stress lives, it can be challenging to sit down with your thoughts, but you must. It is the only way to check in with yourself and see where you are spiritually, mentally, and emotionally. There may be areas that could use improvement or aspects about the seasons that speak to you.

These prompts call for self-examination and intention setting and are organized by the four seasons—spring, summer, autumn, and winter. Just as you grow throughout life, you will grow alongside the seasons. It will be like you are moving through time as we cover each sabbat and season. Each meditation is meant to put you in a state of consciousness and mindfulness so that you may see beyond each day and look into who you are as a witch and as a person. We rarely get time to just *be*. Our attention is commanded elsewhere much of the time. So let the meditations take you away and give you a fresh perspective on your life.

When using the prompts, be as honest as possible, but do not judge your answers. There is power in being truthful with yourself. It makes us stronger and more knowledgeable of who we are, where our limits lie, and what we gravitate toward. May the combination of the meditations and the prompts bring you closer to enlightenment and contentment. Now go forward and explore what this journal has to teach you. *Blessed be.*

SPRING

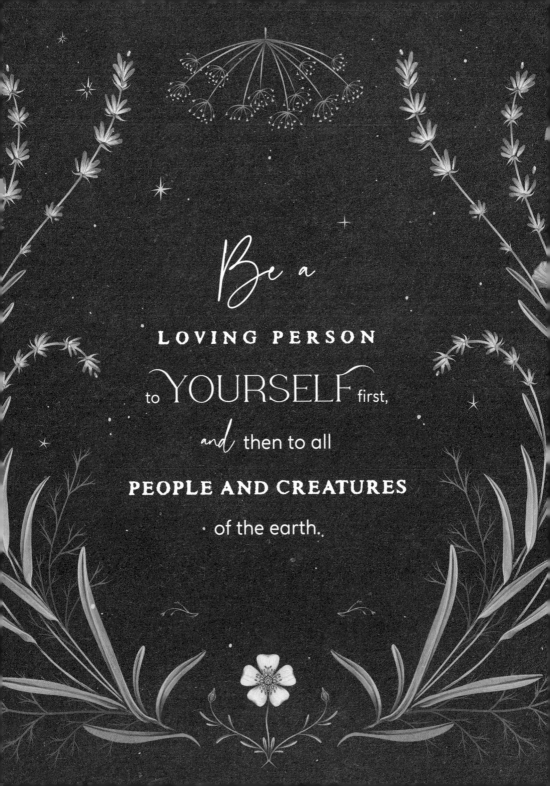

Be a

LOVING PERSON

to YOURSELF first,

and then to all

PEOPLE AND CREATURES

· of the earth. ·

Spring is a time of rebirth. It's the season of starting fresh, starting anew. During this time, we can begin to toss aside what held us back in the winter and instead focus on what we will attain in the spring. Distancing ourselves from the past will help us be more present and leave us free to explore the newer version of ourselves.

What are some things you'd like to let go of? Why do they no longer serve you?

When spring takes over the land, the earth is in her maiden phase. She is just beginning her journey of life and growth. The first vegetation seeds have been planted, and the earth is waking up after her long slumber. A new chapter awaits her when she will finally be able to breathe, shine, and blossom. Think of this time as one of renewal, and become childlike once again.

What aspects of your childhood have shaped you into who you are today?

Flowers need water, attention, sun, and pollination to thrive and bloom. It is a lengthy and slow process, but when a flower finally blooms, it is gorgeous. We are very much like the flower. We must endure hardship, confusion, doubt, and anxiety, but when we finally conquer those obstacles, we are more robust and more beautiful for it.

What hardships have you endured? How are you a better person because of them?

One of the best things about beginnings is that there is so much potential, so many paths one can choose to take. But to do so, one must have direction. Imagine an arrow like that of a compass trying to calibrate where to stop. Now, picture yourself as the arrow and move about. Ask yourself which direction you want to go and where you'd like to end up.

Where does the arrow point? Where do you want to end up, and how will you get there?

Our dreams can be wild, a regurgitation of our waking life or a way for us to hope. This new time of year is perfect to put our desires into motion. Maybe you want a new place to live, a familiar (animal companion), a workshop, or a new cauldron. Now is the perfect time to address your wants and say to the Universe, "This is my wish, so mote it be."

Without judgment, list your hopes and desires for this year. How would they change your life?

Ostara, March 20 to 22, is the Spring Equinox, when the night and day are equally as long. Its arrival heralds a time of rumination and reflection. The shadow loses its hold on the earth to leave room for the Sun to take over and extend the day. We can do so similarly with our shadow self. It is the part of us that we do not wish to see, our unsavory side. Imagine you and your shadow self facing each other. Ask them to give you insight into yourself that you can take with you into the spring. Imagine them handing you a gift with all the lessons inside. Open it, let the lessons come to you, and meditate on them.

What was in the gift box? What lessons has your shadow self taught you?

Tucked in a cave, the mighty grizzly bear awakens from hibernation and stalks back into the natural world. Grizzlies are amazingly powerful creatures who, once roused, can lift boulders, care for their young, and force obstacles out of their way. They're an unstoppable force. Aspire to be like the grizzly, and let nothing stop you.

What is in your way? How will you use your power to move past it?

The Sun hangs highest in the sky. His light shines on everything below, strengthening, fortifying, and satisfying. His power extends to every living creature. Without the Sun, life, as we know it, simply wouldn't exist. Just as we depend on the Sun to help us, it is perfectly all right to rely on those who give us strength and life. It is impossible to do everything on your own. Never forget that everyone needs someone or something to get them through.

Who or what is the Sun in your life? How do they enrich or support you?

Unlike autumn or winter, spring is the time for elation and jubilance. The Sun is making his ascent to full actualization, leaving us to celebrate his verve and our own. And there is so much to be happy and grateful for—the budding flowers, the balmy breeze, the feeling of the sunlight on our skin. Imagine yourself out in nature as you meditate, exploring and rediscovering his beauty.

Name five things you like about spring. What about them makes you happy or excited?

Go to a quiet field or park. Take in the birds singing atop the trees, the feeling of the wind passing over your skin, bees buzzing about, and the grass beneath you. When we're stuck inside all day, it can be easy to forget what lies just outside our doors. We have to connect ourselves to the earth in order to tap into the power of our magic and the scenery Mother Nature has in store for us. When you are able to be outside in a comfortable place, you can just *be*. No fretting about work or seeing someone seemingly more successful show off. Instead, be present.

Name five things you can either hear, taste, smell, feel, or see. How does it feel to pause and take all that in?

Sometimes when emerging from winter, we may feel like we let ourselves go during the cold months, and now that the light of day is on us, our perceived flaws seem starkly evident. When this happens, it can damage our self-confidence and lead us to think we are not as wonderful as we indeed are. Nevertheless, if we give in to these negative thoughts and self-talk, it can interfere with our craft and leak into the other parts of our lives. Instead of meditating on your imperfections, focus on the good and how sublime you are.

What are four of the biggest compliments anyone has given you?

Hummingbirds are an exciting bunch. They are the only birds who can fly backward. They love sugar water, make mouse noises, and are difficult to pin down. But they fly quickly, come in beautiful colors, and are incredible all on their own. The hummingbird doesn't concern itself with the opinions of others but flies as much and as high as it pleases. Our quirks make us who we are, and we should be proud of them. They make us unique in our own right.

What are your quirks? Take any quirk you do not like and turn it into a positive.

Aranyani, the goddess of the forest and its animal inhabitants, wears little bells around her ankles that chime as she dances along the forest floor. She is fearless, elusive, and a pretty great dancer. Aranyani prefers to wander alone to remote places, finding solace in the jungle. If you listen closely to the wind, you can hear the tinkling of her bells. Her free spirit allows her to roam the land and connect with Nature.

Find some greenery around you and dance as Aranyani dances. Be unrestrained and connect with the world around you. How does it feel?

In witchcraft, every color has a specific meaning—black for protection, and green for growth. But in Nature, colors have entirely different meanings. They can signify a poisonous animal or a dying tree, can help us differentiate between male and female creatures, and draw the eye's attention. Colors can also affect our moods negatively or positively. Without them, our world would be much bleaker.

What is your favorite color to use in your spellwork?

Water is an essential element in Nature but also in us. It represents our deepest and shallowest emotions. Just like our feelings, water can be calm or tempestuous. When our reservoirs are low or running dry, our lives can be spasmodic, causing us to feel upended. It is imperative to keep our reservoirs as full as possible to keep us in tune with our emotions and craft. Water is necessary for a better quality of life.

Open your third eye and picture your reservoirs. How full or empty are they? If running low, what can you do to replenish your emotional waters?

Bees, an integral part of our ecosystem, are mighty insects. They are always working, always on the run, continuously moving the community forward. A bee can do quite a bit alone, but he can do so much more with the hive. When a bee is in trouble, he knows the hive can provide guidance and protection to one another. When doubt or obstacles come into play, it is vital to lean on your tribe. Sometimes all we have is each other.

Who is in your community? How do you all support each other?

At times, the prospects of the new year can be overwhelming. So many things can go right, but they can also go wrong. Because of the unknown, we may get stressed and want to hide from our fears. But this is not the way. As witches, we face what we fear, go into the unknown, and come out the other side wiser than before. Rather than being afraid or anxious, take a moment to breathe and sit with your thoughts. Will your worries actually come true? Most likely not. We cannot predict the future, but we can influence it with our positive thinking.

List your apprehensions for the upcoming year, then ask yourself, "What if everything works out all right?" Use this to challenge yourself to see what good can come from your fears.

The elusive deer is a ubiquitous animal for a good reason. Deer are peaceful herbivore creatures who roam the forest, living their lives. Though quiet, deer can also be warriors. The gallant stag fights for his space and his mate with his antlers. This duality makes the deer an interesting animal to observe and make your totem. They move with the wisdom of the forest and the freedom of Nature.

What is your animal totem? What do you like about it, and why did you pick that particular one?

Beltane, May 30, is a day of joy and celebration for being alive and for all of Nature's creations. By this point, summer is just around the corner, and with that comes a complete awakening of the earth. Though life is stressful for any witch, this is the time to forget it all, commemorate this holy day, and be grateful for what has been bestowed upon us by the Universe. Life is fleeting, so why not party?

Name at least three aspects of your life that you love, and three gifts Nature has given you.

SUMMER

This is a

TIME TO EMPHASIZE

JOY, ABUNDANCE,

and the CONNECTION

of all living things.

CELEBRATE THE LIFE-GIVING

SUN—intoxicating and vibrant,

warm and fertile.

The ocean waves roll and fizzle on the shore. The Sun sets in the sky, leaving behind brilliant orange, pink, and yellow hues. Sand gets in between your toes as you stroll the beach, and a feeling comes over you. Nothing else exists besides you and the Sun. The moment he leaves the day for the night, you feel free and infinite. As you should, because you are the same. You are comprised of endless possibilities. Focus on what you are capable of and the freedom within you.

Take a moment to explore your possibilities. Let your mind wander to what you can accomplish and how to use your powers, then write it down.

The life of a witch constantly moves with the seasons, not just Halloween. There is just as much to do in the summer as in the autumn. So much so that we might get caught up in the go, go, go of the season. After being seemingly held back, we are now in the most open and active time of the year. But even in this busy time, we still must slow down and make time for ourselves, whether that means relaxing in a quiet space or brewing up potions. What matters most is always you.

How do you slow down after a hectic time? What is your version of self-care, and how does it help you?

Witchcraft is a path of discipline, study, experimentation, and mystique. It is a lifestyle, but even so, there are occasions when it can become strict and all-consuming. Even with the essential parts of our lives, it is crucial to simply enjoy ourselves. If you feel yourself becoming too preoccupied with anything, take a moment to ask yourself, "Am I enjoying myself?" If the answer is yes, keep doing it! Spirit also delights in our contentment, so we should honor it and ourselves by carving out some delectation.

What are some activities you find pleasure in? Be specific about what makes them enjoyable.

Actualization is when the dreams or goals we have come true. It is a feeling of accomplishment on our hard work and success, or it can be as enthralling and straightforward as being at the right place at the right time. What contributes to actualization is having the desire, creating pathways for that desire to manifest, and letting the Universe do the rest. Though having our wishes fulfilled is what we all want, it should not be dwelled upon. Instead, take this moment to release any lingering worry or anxiety. Let it lift off you, and leave everything up to the gods.

Have you been able to let go of any unease? What other aspects of your life can you focus on instead?

Similar to the Full Moon, summer is also a time of immense energy. In the vibrancy of the tree leaves, the strong current of the rivers, and the lively air of the people, there is so much to draw from. Because of this special time of year, your goals and aspirations have a better chance of coming true, if they haven't already. Sit in a quiet place outside, and imagine the energy surrounding you is like mist. Then let it envelop you, feeling it on your skin, and let yourself be emboldened by it.

What does this season inspire you to do? When was the last time you were truly inspired?

Midsummer, June 20 to 22, is when summer has officially arrived. It is also known as the Fire Festival. This day is all about celebrating the Sun and acknowledging that, after the holy day, the Sun wanes in power and appearance. It is a peaceful transition toward autumn. Imagine yourself as big and as bright as the Sun during this time. Take in all your power, and pull from the resources around you. Allow yourself to be whole.

Now that you have tapped into your power, what will you do with it? How do you want to express it?

During summer, the earth is in a state of maturity—i.e., motherhood. With motherhood comes the ability to create, nurture, teach, be strong, and advocate for others. You do not have to be a mother to possess these qualities as a witch. Because we are of the earth, everyone can possess her qualities.

Which qualities do you share with Mother Nature?

The yarrow flower, which looks similar to a daisy, is deceptively delicate. But what most do not realize is that it is actually quite persistent. Regardless of whether the soil it grows in is ideal or not, the yarrow flower persists. No matter what life throws our way, we must persevere. Not only is it in our nature, but it is also required to advance and grow. The yarrow flower promotes courage and confidence. Whatever adverse conditions you are going through, remember to persist. You can do it. You always have.

For you to be where you are right now, you had to have gone through good and bad situations. What are some of the difficult periods you have endured? How did you get past them, and how will you persevere now?

In the Ojibwe culture, there are tales of Nanabozho the rabbit. Nanabozho is a trickster and a shapeshifter. It can turn into any human or animal, regardless of gender. This nature is what allows Nanabozho to gather so many unique perspectives. Because Nanabozho can expand and shift, it is able to add to its wealth of knowledge. Though humans do not possess this power, we still can be like Nanabozho if we keep an open mind and surround ourselves with different situations and people. That is how we shape our minds and our whole beings.

Picture yourself as a shapeshifter. What or who would you turn into? What would you hope to learn from that experience?

The fringe tree, though it sprouts in summer, looks like snow decorating its branches. The petals of its pretty white flowers can sometimes hang as though melancholy, but they hide the fact that they will sprout purple fruit in the autumn. There are moments in life when things are not always as they appear. You have to look closer and let go of any preconceived notions to see more. When you do, you open yourself up to nuance and possibilities.

What are some assumptions you have made? What did you learn when you discovered the truth?

Every living being has an aura, an energy field surrounding them. It is something we all innately possess. When we feel good, our auras are strong and more extensive. When we feel weak or distressed, it shrinks and clings closer to the body. Thankfully, there is a way to cleanse it with both physical and spiritual methods. Go outside, especially on a windy day, and stand firm and tall. Open your arms wide as if you are receiving a gift. Throw your head back and feel the wind move all over you, blowing away all the impurities in your aura until you are thoroughly purified.

Mentally, we can also cleanse our auras with positive self-talk. Identify what is causing your aura to get "dirty," then write down which words or phrases you can use to cleanse it.

Summer has a reputation for being full of fun and luxury. Everyone is outside enjoying life, but sometimes with that comes odd feelings of dissatisfaction and insecurities. "I wish I was having as much fun as them." When this happens, it can be so effortless to give up and compare our lives and experiences to others. Instead, it is important to remember to focus on ourselves. We are just as capable of having fun if we narrow our attention to what *we* love and stick with that.

How can you fill your life with fun and pleasures?

Lammas, August 1 or 2, is a day of harvest. During this time, we reap and enjoy what we have sown. The wonderful thing about this day is its duality. The Sun is still out, but he dwindles. We have just harvested, but whispers of autumn slowly crescendo. We celebrate the fruits of summer but acknowledge it is coming to an end. It is this duality that also exists in us. Like the earth, we contain so many possibilities and contradictions. Sit with this thought and know that dualism is not only normal, but *right*.

Write down some of your perfect contradictions. If you feel strange about any of them, also explore why.

Like mating season in Nature, summer is when everyone comes out with their best looks to attract others. In the day and age of social media, this is increased a hundredfold. There are so many ways to access and see attractive people with their partners or friends. This, in turn, can leave us feeling insecure about our appearance or our relationship status. We are all doing the best we can to enjoy the life we have. Find comfort in knowing the people you envy might be just as uncertain. We are all doing the best we can. So instead of being resentful, focus on you and the stunning person you are.

Name at least five of your enviable attributes, whether abstract or physical.

Though this season is the motherhood stage, many of us feel as though we are still in our adolescent phase. Perhaps you feel awkward or uncomfortable or not fully yourself, and that is perfectly fine. That is a part of life, and instead of having a negative interpretation, think of it as a transitionary period. We learn so much in our youth, so embrace this time as you process all of your changes.

How different are you now than you were a year ago? Five years ago?

At times it can be challenging to think outside of ourselves and our day-to-day lives, but today open your mind and go on a meditative adventure. Wherever you are, take a good look at your surroundings and briefly memorize them enough to envision everything with your mind. Close your eyes and let your consciousness drift out of your body and into the air. Ascend until you are away from your space and look at what's around you with your third eye. Keep going until you can see the rooftops of buildings, people walking by who are slowly turning into ants, the vehicles moving about on the road. Drift into the sky until you pass right through a cloud until your location becomes one of many. Go higher until you see your home country, then continent, then planet. You are a small piece that makes up the entire Universe. Know it and be freed because of it. Now, slowly come back down until you come back into yourself.

How was the ride? What revelations did you have, and what did you discover?

Guanyin is a revered Chinese goddess of mercy and compassion in the Buddhist tradition. Her spirit was warm and kind, despite the way others treated her. According to her tale, she was killed by her father and sent to hell, but her gentle ways endeared her to her people. Their adoration made a trying situation more bearable for her. Like Guanyin, we can also practice kindness and gentleness toward others and ourselves, to everyone's benefit.

Think of a time when someone has been kind to you. How did they help you? Now, what are some ways you can pass that along to others?

It is often said that happiness is elusive. The harder you try to grab on to it, the farther it floats out of your reach. But that does not mean you have to sit and wait for it. Felicity can arrive in many unexpected ways, but we do often know what makes us happy. For this meditation, surround yourself with as many delightful things as possible. Close your eyes, then let your mind drift to what makes you smile, what makes you laugh, or who is your favorite person. Let the sweet, warm feeling overtake you like a blanket on a winter's night. Feel yourself relax and let your lips curl up.

List three objects or activities that make you happy, then list three people who make your heart soar.

AUTUMN

When the

LENGTH OF NIGHT AND

DAY STRIKE A PERFECTLY

EQUAL BALANCE,

greet this time of transition

with an extreme focus on

centering the self.

Somewhere deep in the forest, a circle of mushrooms lies, appearing seemingly out of nowhere. German folklore says that when mushrooms appear like this, it is a sign that witches have been dancing on the forest floor in celebration and preparation for Samhain. The Witches' Ring is living proof that our joy, no matter how seemingly small or insignificant, leaves an impression not only on the Universe but also on the people around us.

What are some moments of happiness that have impacted you? It can be your joy or someone else's.

Snakes tend to have a negative reputation, but in reality, they are one of the most adaptable and fascinating creatures on this earth. They are independent, strong, clever, and fierce. As an animal totem, snakes bring creation, change, and help getting rid of old habits. Part of witchcraft is gazing past what is seemingly bad and looking for the good.

Take this moment to reflect on your misconceptions and look past them. Have you ever been confronted with the truth about an incorrect perception?

Strength is a quality all of us want. We are told to be strong in the face of adversity, but we tend to think strength means being completely self-sufficient. In truth, no one can completely do everything themselves. The tall, hardwood birch tree stands firm in the comfort of the forest and with its group. Yet even with these qualities, the birch tree relies on toadstool mushrooms to provide nutrients. It is a symbiotic relationship. It does not mean the birch tree is weak, nor does it mean the toadstool is stronger than the birch. Despite everything, we all could use a little aid.

Do you struggle with accepting help? What prevents you from doing so?

Once autumn takes hold of the earth, everything slows down. Not as many animals move about, and they prepare for hibernation as the weather cools. This deceleration affects us as well. When we are able to pause, we are forced to be in the present moment. Gaze at the wind shuffling the leaves outside. Listen for the birds. Look at the water still on the lake's glassy surface. Close your eyes, and sit in stillness and solitude. Open your mind to whatever thoughts surface and let them change.

Reflect on what came to you. Did you get any insights?

The Sun has descended, and the Moon is out in her full glory. The heart opens when there is nothing outside other than the silver moonlight. It is the vulnerability of the night. Unlike the darkness of the unknown, it is the darkness of safety. Without the exposing light of the Sun, the light of the Moon allows us to know we are all right and we can share our deepest secrets. On a late night, invite someone to sit and talk with you. Be open about whatever is on your mind and listen to the other person. When the light of day eventually comes, you will be much stronger and lighter.

Describe your night. What did you share? How did it feel to share?

Mabon, September 20 to 22, is the Autumnal Equinox. It is the other day of the year when day and night are perfectly balanced, yet it signals the diminishing power of the Sun and ushers in the dark season. This day is also the Witches' Thanksgiving. The Witches' New Year approaches quickly, which means new adventures and being grateful to the past for bringing you into the future.

List two things you are grateful for, then list two things you are looking forward to in the new year.

When the leaves change, it is time to seek shelter and spend time with those who make you feel warm inside. One of the most beautiful things about autumn is the season of community. The upcoming harvest and the holidays bring a special sense of magic in the air. Share this time with someone you really love. Honor yourself with socialization and bless others with your company.

Who do you like to spend time with? How do they enrich your life?

Redwoods are the tallest and oldest trees on earth. They can grow as tall as 379 feet and as old as 2,200 years. They are partly keepers of this earth and have seen many of our lifetimes. What is so fantastic about these redwoods is their ability to stand the test of time. From the day they were planted to now, they have seen it all. They hold secrets we cannot begin to know. Founders like the redwoods remind us of our ancestry, of people who have come before and know much. Lean on older loved ones. They have much to teach.

Who is the "redwood" in your life? What can they still teach you? What have you learned from them over the years?

Just as summer is the earth's motherhood stage, autumn is the
beginning of her Crone stage. A Crone is an older, wiser woman.
Because she has experienced much, the Crone knows who she is and
is secure in her power. Donned in dark autumn colors, she does not
have to prove herself to anyone. Instead, she moves about bringing
knowledge and advice to those who ask. She does not bend to
pressure; she simply *is*. Open your third eye and ask the Crone for her
wisdom. Keep your senses open for anything she has to say.

What did she tell you? How will you apply this new information?

Leaves from differing trees turn varying colors of yellow, rusty browns, and orange. Each color represents various qualities. Focus on the orange leaves in particular. Orange represents ambition, building energy, creativity, emotional healing, health, and warmth. Surround yourself with orange items, take one of these attributes, and apply it to your meditation.

Which attribute did you meditate on? What realizations did you have?

On a muted day, clouds cover the breadth of the sky. They inadvertently give off a dreary look, making some witches depressed. But on the other hand, the clouds give a softer hue to the environment. Every day cannot be sunny, so the clouds are for those who favor the in between, the gray and nuanced. As witches, we exist in transitionary spaces constantly. Change is good, even if it may not appear so at first. After all, the Sun is always waiting at the end of a cloudy day.

Name some of the gray areas in your life. Do you like that they are gray, or would you prefer black or white?

Brown, the color of the earth, is ubiquitous. It is the color of our food, the land, the leaves, many animals, and many of our people. It is closely linked to clarity of thought, stability, and feeling grounded. Surround yourself and decorate your altar with brown items and ruminate on its meaning. The colors around us tell us so much more than just their outward appearance.

What does brown mean to you? What about its meanings sticks with you?

Samhain, October 31, is the first holy day on the witches' calendar and the final harvest. What makes this sabbat unique is that the veil between worlds—the living and the dead or any parallel universes—is the thinnest, lending us the opportunity to communicate with our ancestors and those who have passed. It is a time to celebrate life as we know it and the lives of those who came before us. Think about your life in its current state. Then go further back and think of your parents and their parents and your extended family, and see we are all connected.

Who do you want to talk to on this holiday? What will you say to them?

When the rain pours across the land, everything halts. The animals go into hiding, and we look for a dry place to rest. Though the rain can be frustrating, it is a blessing on its own. Everything stills as the rain nourishes the earth. Droplets make pitter-patter sounds on the roof and the windowpanes. All is calm. A forced rest might be an inconvenience at times, but it can also be precisely what is needed. Stop thinking, doing, or moving, and enjoy this moment.

Write a letter to the rain, telling it how you spend your restful period.

Out in space the stars of the Milky Way lie. They are giant celestial bodies that reside light-years away from us, yet we are connected. As people, but especially as witches, we are tied to the stars and their alignments with the Sun and Earth. They influence us in our birth charts, partially because we are made of the same matter. They speak to us. On a starry night, look up and know you share the same sky.

What amazes you about the vastness of space?

Family is everything, whether biological, adopted, or chosen. It is the very foundation on which we are born and where we are molded. When off on our own, forgetting that familial connection happens every day. We may be focused on who we are in our professional lives and may get lost in the shuffle. Return to your roots as a way to get insight into who you are and your place in the world. If nothing else, family will tell you who you are.

What is your family structure like? What do you like best about your family? What have they taught you?

The red squirrel hurriedly climbs the trunk of its home. She brings with her some food for her children. In witchcraft, the squirrel represents patience, thoughtfulness, and endurance. She does not need the affirmation or approval of others to be as kind as she is. Like the squirrel, we may also benefit from patience and endurance as we wait out this colder season for the warmer ones ahead.

Describe which areas you can be more patient in. More thoughtful?

Autumn and maturity go hand in hand. The youthful days are gone, and now there is time to look back on the past year and look forward to the future. Besides being a wise woman, the Crone is nostalgic as well. All the delights and despairs of the year are in the forefront of the mind, but there is hope and wonder for the future.

Name some delights of the past year. Now some despairs. What was the year like for you so far, and what do you look forward to?

Winter is just around the corner. Take a look at the world around you. The bare trees, the disposition of your peers, the changes hidden in the air. This is the last stint of change before the darkest portion of the dark season. So much good has come before it, and good will come during and after. There is no need to fear. Instead, thank the Spirits for all they have given you during the season, and rest assured, knowing you will be given more in the future.

What are your plans for winter? What knowledge are you taking with you?

WINTER

LOVE

PEACE THAT DWELLS

in this SEASON.

It is a time of

RESTORATIVE DARKNESS AND

DEEP DREAMING.

Pine cones may seem like simple decorations, but they are far from it. With their layered appearance, pine cones are suitable for protecting the seeds of a pine tree. The layers prevent its contents from being damaged by the cold or wind. In Nature, protection is everything. Animals fight over protection and have to shield themselves from other animals daily, yet this is their way of life—as it is for witches. But witches have the control to protect ourselves from the evil lurking about. We carry with us the strength to overcome whatever obstacle we face.

Do you have belongings or people you protect like the pine cone? Who/what are they? What would happen if you stopped protecting them?

Snow falls on every building, tree, and house. The air steams as people talk in quick voices, shivering from the cold. The Sun sets earlier and earlier every day. All the while, we are stuck inside. They call it stir-crazy, when it feels more like suffocation. Because we are guided by Nature, it is easy to feel stifled while inside, waiting for the cold to subside. But there are moments we must remain indoors. Being restricted from the outside world does not mean there is no way to feel as free. Sit quietly, close your eyes, and open your third eye. Imagine the world around you melting away, and visualize yourself in a picturesque scene. Stay there for as long as you like.

Where would you like to be right now? What would you do the first moment you arrive?

During winter, the earth is in her full-blown Crone phase. As the Crone, she has lived through so much and now has the time to look back on her gains and losses. Most importantly, she does not focus on her losses or use them as a way to bring herself down. Instead, she treats them as lessons she may carry into the next life. For her wins, she celebrates them and is grateful for them. In the end, all that is left is time.

Looking back on the year, what would have made it better? What was the best part of the year?

With all the time one has in this final stage, it is crucial to take stock of what has happened and look ahead. There is not always a clear path forward with any journey, but if it were clean, we would learn nothing. Instead, life twists and turns like tree branches, moving about in different directions. Because we do not know the full scope of our stories, the events of our lives can seem haphazard. But that is why this downtime is much needed. Once the past is behind us, the best that can be done is to use what has stood out and move forward into a brighter future.

Armed with the wisdom of this past year, how will you apply it to the next calendar year?

The wood in the hearth is set. A match has been lit, and now there is a crackling fire. Fire keeps us warm on a cold winter's night, but so does love. They both hold warmth and vitality in them, giving us strength and courage. Snuggle with a loved one near a fire. Savor their touch against yours. Cling to them as if you were trying to commit them to memory. Then enjoy their presence, and thank them for all they do for you.

Who did you choose to snuggle with? What is your relationship to them? What does their love mean to you?

Yule, December 20 to 22, is when the Sun is still in the sky and is on the cusp of regaining strength. Though this day occurs during the dark season, it is a symbol that the Sun will return to full glory, moving the Wheel of Time. The wheel constantly turns, moving us forward in our lives regardless of our path or the obstacles. Whatever you are going through on this sabbat, know time will help it pass.

If you could control the Wheel of Time, what would you do with that power?

In the dark season, most colors blend together—a combination of white and the muted colors of the earth. Overall, the plant life has gone to sleep for the season, yet not all of them have. Winter heathers, elongated flowers that look similar to lavender, bloom despite the harsher conditions. Their hues stand out in the garden. Unlike other flowers, they thrive in the cold. Not everyone is the same, and we all grow better under different climates. Tell yourself it is all right if you do not feel as though you fit in. Perhaps you are not in a suitable atmosphere.

Which environment do you thrive in? What elements do you need to thrive?

We are familiar with the Moon and her phases. But one often gets overlooked: the Dark Moon. In this phase, Mother Moon has returned to her amniotic state. She is in the process of being reborn. The Dark Moon sits in the sky for about one and a half to three and a half days before transitioning to the New Moon. In this period, there is no waiting, no doing, nothing. All the Moon has to do is let her transformation happen.

What do you need rest from? How can you give yourself the time to do nothing?

There is more time to think and get oneself together during the quiet months. Because of this, there is time to take stock of who you do and do not want in your life. In general, we tend to stay in unfulfilling relationships because of shared history or fear of the unknown. That does nothing but hold us back. In order to better our lives, letting go of those who are toxic to us is one of the first steps. You do not owe anyone your time and attention.

Have you ever cut off a toxic person? If so, how did it feel? If not, who would you like to be rid of?

On an early winter morning, fog has blanketed everyone's vision. Instead of a clear view, there is a misty barrier. When this happens, it means the clouds have made their way down to the earth. What seems like a spooky development is actually a marvel. Not everything is as it seems, and at times, we may judge too quickly. The fog eventually lifts and all is back to normal. There is nothing frightening about it.

Remember a time when you misjudged a situation. What was your initial thought? What was the truth?

Though this season is not the most energetic, that does not mean there cannot be room for adventure. Part of being a witch is to explore and experience. When we do this, we not only improve our magic, but we also enrich our lives. Never let the adventurer in you die. There is much to do and see as long as we are alive. And it is our duty to see it.

Have you ever taken an adventure in poor conditions? Where did you go? What was the best part?

The Sun rises, bringing in the dawn. While the earth is mainly covered in darkness, the snow leopard is hunting. Snow leopards are very much loners. They will only leave their shelters during the dawn and early morning, then again at dusk and the evening. It moves about living its life without wanting to be seen. Many of us live our lives this way as well. We are told to socialize when it simply is not in our nature. Know that there is nothing wrong with solitude. If that is what brings peace, so be it.

Do you enjoy solitude? Why or why not? Do you prefer to be around others or on your own?

Candlemas, February 1 or 2, is a sabbat of inspiration. The first seeds of the year are planted and will bloom in the spring. There is a level of magic in the air during this precious time. The unknown may be scary because we are unaware of the outcome of our actions. But the unknown can be a good thing. Planting these seeds of inspiration and sending them into the hands of the Universe means future events might be better than what we can imagine. For this holiday, let yourself dream and be creative.

What is the worst that could go wrong? Try not to dwell on it too much. Now, what is the best that can go right? Dwell on this a little longer.

Water is a fantastical element. It has three states of matter: gas, liquid, and solid. It can erode giant rocks and force its way into any space. When contained, water takes the shape of whatever container it is in. If you try to hold water, you can only do it for so long before it drips out of your hand. Some witches are governed by this element, and for good reason. It is so versatile that it can be anything. Regardless of your elemental sign, think of yourself as water. Focus on how it ebbs and flows, stills and thrashes, and then take that on yourself.

Are you fluid like water, or are you a tad rigid like ice? If the latter, what would it take for you to become more flexible?

Despite this less busy time of the year, there is still much to be done, whether it is school, work, or family. Though those things are essential, they are not as important as time for yourself. Too often we must put aside our feelings and well-being to survive the day. But stillness and awareness are necessary to become the best witch you can possibly be. Carve out time for yourself to do whatever it is you want. Be present in that moment and enjoy yourself. You deserve it.

What did you end up doing? How long has it been since you were able to engage in it?

As quiet befalls the land, all that can be seen is snow, whether on a mountaintop or dusting the ground. It is the earth's way of having a fresh start. The color white is a stand-in for and comprised of all colors. This means it has many possibilities to become anything. In your mind's eye, cloak yourself in white and imagine yourself being renewed and ready for anything you may encounter. You are made anew.

What possibilities do you see for yourself?

The key to birth is death, but not necessarily in the physical sense. The dark season serves as the earth's resting period in life and in death. For the next cycle to start, the current one must end. But do not be afraid, because positive change is on the way if you are willing to let go of what no longer serves you. Put them aside, and do not pick them back up again. They will only hold you back from your destiny.

What do you need to let go of? Why were you holding on to it?

You have persevered through another year. You have worked so hard on yourself, and now that winter is coming to an end, it is time to reflect on all you have accomplished. Focus on the moments you felt on top of the world, the moments you were so proud of yourself, and any growth in your personal life and in your magical journey.

List your top five shining moments this year. What do these say about you?